For Roger, Michael, Hannah,
and our precious angel in heaven, Roger Thomas II.
You have all given me my wings and helped me fly.

MOOKI'S SECRET
published by Gold 'n' Honey Books
a division of Multnomah Publishers, Inc.
and in association with the literary agency of Dupree/Miller & Associates

© 1998 by Kari Smalley Gibson and Gary Smalley
Illustrations © 1998 by Richard Bernal
Designed by Kirk DouPonce

International Standard Book Number: 1-57673-266-5

Gold 'n' Honey is a trademark of Multnomah Publishers, Inc.,
and is registered in the U.S. Patent and Trademark Office.

Printed in the United States of America

For information:
MULTNOMAH PUBLISHERS, INC.
POST OFFICE BOX 1720
SISTERS, OREGON 97759

98 99 00 01 02 03 04 — 10 9 8 7 6 5 4 3 2 1

Forest Tales

Mooki's Secret

KARI SMALLEY GIBSON with GARY SMALLEY

Illustrated by

RICHARD BERNAL

GOLD 'N' HONEY BOOKS • SISTERS, OREGON

$\mathcal{M}$ooki frowned as he looked up at the big house. Was this *really* going to be his new home? Critters who didn't have families lived here. Mooki squinted at the sign above the door as he read the words:

Welcome Home.

Mooki's eyes filled with tears. *This wasn't his home.* Mooki had lost his home when a flood washed his house away, and his family with it. A kind field mouse had taken him in, but before long Mooki grew too big for the mouse's tiny house.

Swoosh! The front door swung open and out stepped the biggest critter Mooki had ever seen. She had a long nose and her golden eyes sparkled with kindness.

"Hello, Mooki," said Mrs. Twizzer as she wiped her hands on her apron. "We are so excited that you've finally arrived. How was your trip?"

Mooki looked up at her loving face. Mrs. Twizzer seemed very nice, but all Mooki could do was mumble, "Mmm, mmm."

You see, Mooki had a problem, and he wanted to keep it to himself. It was his big secret and he wasn't going to let anyone find out.

For the next few days, Mooki avoided the other critters who lived in Mrs. Twizzer's house. Mooki wanted to keep his problem a secret. If anyone tried to talk to Mooki, he would cover his mouth and turn away. But he knew he couldn't hide his secret forever.

Mrs. Twizzer was very kind to Mooki. She seemed to understand that something was bothering him. Several times he almost talked to her about his secret. But he couldn't quite bring himself to do it.

One warm evening the critters decided to sleep on the front porch where it was cooler. Mooki joined them, but he put his pillow in a quiet corner, a safe distance away. Soon the rest of the critters were telling jokes.

"What's black and white and red all over?" asked Tippy.

"A newspaper?" Gibby guessed.

"No," said Tippy smugly.

The others yelled out their answers, everyone except Mooki.

"No!" Tippy replied. "You're all wrong! I'll tell you what's black and white and red all over. It's *Stinker*—right after Mrs. Twizzer caught him with his paw in the strawberry jam!" They all burst out laughing. Even Mooki opened his mouth and laughed so hard that he rolled right off his pillow.

"Wowsy!" cried Tippy. "Look at those humongous teeth!"

Everyone stared at Mooki in surprise.

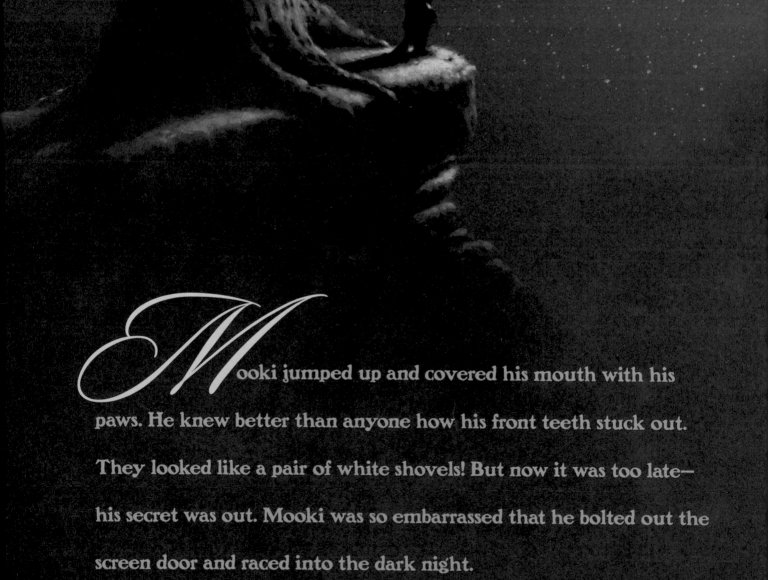

*M*ooki jumped up and covered his mouth with his

paws. He knew better than anyone how his front teeth stuck out.

They looked like a pair of white shovels! But now it was too late—

his secret was out. Mooki was so embarrassed that he bolted out the

screen door and raced into the dark night.

"Why do I have these awful teeth?" sobbed Mooki as he ran.

"I hate being different!" Finally he flopped down under an oak tree.

As he tried to catch his breath, big teardrops fell from his eyes onto

the grass—*drip, splat, drip.* He looked up at the stars, but their

twinkles were blurred by his tears. He didn't think the hurt in his

heart would ever go away.

After that night, Mooki kept to himself. He avoided talking to

the other critters because he didn't want them to see his horribly

huge teeth. Mooki's heart felt heavy and sad as he watched the

other critters giggle and chat, but he never joined in.

very day before school started,

Mooki watched the other critters play stick-nut in

the meadow. It looked like such a thrilling game—

how Mooki longed to play! The critters from Mrs.

Twizzer's home had a team called the Shooting

Stars. *Oh,* Mooki thought, *if only I could be a*

Shooting Star too!

One morning, Mooki stood on the sidelines and

watched as the Shooting Stars played a very

exciting game. The score was tied. But just as

Payton darted for the hollow log, the nut thumped

him right on the head!

The game stopped while the team helped poor Payton off the field. Then Gibby, the team captain, looked around for another player to replace Payton. And he looked right at Mooki!

Mooki's heart did a somersault! Then he stepped out onto the field. Could it be? Was Gibby *really* going to ask Mooki to play?

"Don't pick Mooki!" chirped Payton. "He'll make us lose for sure. No one can possibly run with teeth like that!"

All the other critters started laughing.

"Yeah, look at those chompers!" howled Mikey.

"They're so enormous," added Stinker.

"What a wacky set of teeth!" squeaked Gregory.

ooki turned and ran, not wanting to hear another word. He dashed into the woods as fast as his short legs could go, his eyes blurred by tears. He ran and ran until he couldn't go another step, and then he plopped down next to a gurgling creek. He had never gone this deep into the woods before. He was sure that he was terribly lost.

"This is the worst day of my life!" sobbed Mooki as he stared at his reflection in the water. "I'm *never* going back!"

Just then, something burst out of the water and yelled, *"Never?"*

Mooki was so shocked, he fell right into the creek. **Ker-splash!**

When Mooki's head came out of the water, he was met by an explosion of giggles. He opened his eyes to see what was making all the racket. And there in front of him was a furry little critter that looked a lot like he did. Only this little critter had a big grin on her face.

"What will you never do again?" she asked.

"Who are you?" exclaimed Mooki.

"My name is Suzzi," she answered. "Are you lost?"

"Maybe," said Mooki with a little sniffle as he climbed onto the shore. "My name is Mooki."

"You look sad, Mooki," said Suzzi. "Would you like some acorn cookies? My mom makes the very best!"

*L*ook what I found in the creek!" called Suzzi as she and Mooki approached a lodge home made of sticks and branches. More little critters scampered out and gathered around Mooki. And they all looked a lot like he did, too!

"This is my new friend Mooki," announced Suzzi with a toothy grin.

Suzzi's mom set a plateful of acorn cookies on the table. "It's nice to meet you, Mooki," said Mrs. Chomper. "Please, have some cookies."

"What brings you out to this part of the woods, Mooki?" asked Mr. Chomper.

"The truth is, I ran away," said Mooki sadly. "I just don't fit in with the other critters where I live. They tease me about my teeth." Mooki looked around at Suzzi and her family. "And I can see that your teeth are sort of like mine, but—" He opened his mouth to show them—"my teeth are *enormous!*"

"Mooki," said Mr. Chomper, "do you know what sort of folks you come from?"

Mooki shook his head sadly. "I haven't seen my family since I was just a little guy."

*M*ooki," said Mrs. Chomper, "you belong to the *beaver* family! Just like us."

"And beavers must chew wood every day," explained Mr. Chomper. "That's what keeps our teeth healthy and strong."

"If you don't chew your wood," warned Suzzi, "your teeth will grow long and crooked! And they won't be very pretty."

Then Suzzi's family led Mooki down to the water to teach him how to chew wood properly. They also showed him how to make tremendous noises by smacking his big, flat tail.

It was great to be a beaver! And it felt wonderful to sink his teeth into a fresh piece of wood. Mooki had never been so happy!

"You see, Mooki, we're all different," explained Mrs. Chomper. "Moose have enormous horns, lizards have buggy eyes, and goats have furry beards. Being different is what makes us special."

"Mooki, want to know another reason why it's awesome to have beaver teeth?" asked Suzzi with a wide grin. "You can chew over 300 trees in a year!"

"Wow, that's a lot of trees!" Mooki gave his tail a loud whack and laughed.

efore they left the creek, Mrs. Chomper placed a comforting paw on Mooki's shoulder. "Mooki, I always tell my kits that if someone makes fun of them, it might be because they have an owie in their heart. Sometimes when folks feel hurt or sad, they say mean things. It's just their way to hide the hurt they're feeling."

Mooki put his paw over his heart. He knew how it felt to hurt inside. Mooki's hurts made him lonely. And sometimes they made him angry too.

"If critters make fun of your teeth," said Mr. Chomper, "think about why they are teasing you. Maybe they have a hurt so big that they can't say anything kind."

Mooki nodded. "I'll try to remember that. Thank you for everything. I should go home now. I know Mrs. Twizzer will be worried about me."

"Come visit us again," called Mrs. Chomper.

$\mathscr{S}$uzzi walked Mooki back through the woods until the surroundings became familiar to him again. Then she handed him a small wood carving of a beaver family.

"Now, if anyone teases you about your teeth or about being

different," said Suzzi, "you just look at this and remember that you're just like us. You're a beaver and you're special!"

"It's beautiful," said Mooki quietly. "Thanks for everything, Suzzi."

"I'm sure glad I found you in the creek, Mooki." She laughed, then waved good-bye. "Come back and visit us again soon."

"You bet!" yelled Mooki as he watched her walk back into the woods.

As Mooki approached the meadow, he saw Gibby trying to crack open an acorn with a rock. It looked like he was having a tough time.

"Hey, do you need any help?" Mooki called out.

Gibby nodded toward a tall pile of acorns. "All these nuts need to be opened for tomorrow's game. But the nutshells are harder than granite. Grab a rock if you want to help out, Mooki."

"Oh, I've got something even better than a rock," replied Mooki. He placed an acorn between his teeth and bit down hard. *Crack! Crunch!* The shell fell off like magic.

"Wow!" said Gibby. "That was great!"

"I guess I'll have to be the stick-nut nutcracker," Mooki answered, laughing.

Gibby beamed. "How about being a Shooting Star instead?"

"Sure, that would be great!" exclaimed Mooki.

Later that evening, Mooki showed Mrs. Twizzer and the other critters the small carving that Suzzi had given him. "You see, I'm part of the beaver family," he explained with fresh confidence. "And now I'm not ashamed of my teeth."

"You have a beautiful smile, Mooki," said Mrs. Twizzer.

Mooki smiled a big toothy smile. And suddenly he realized that the hurt in his heart was gone.

Small Talk

with Gary Smalley

The Gift of Trust

Parents, it's my hope that you'll use the ideas in SmallTalk to speak with your child about inner feelings. It's not at all unusual for young children to experience painful feelings of shame or embarrassment about being "different" in one way or another. Reading *Mooki's Secret* together may bring those feelings to the surface and generate a teachable moment.

After you've read *Mooki's Secret*, ask your child:

- *How did Mooki feel when his secret was discovered?*

- *What did Mooki do when he was teased about his teeth?*

- *Did you ever feel bad after someone teased you?*

- *How did Suzzi's family encourage Mooki?*

- *What good things did Mooki learn about himself?*

- *What good things have you learned about yourself?*

Point out to your child that the Chomper family helped Mooki see that his teeth were good and special. Their warm acceptance and encouragement helped Mooki get past the painful stage of feeling strange, different, and ashamed. We can encourage our children in similar ways.

It is so important for you to help your child understand that we all experience painful things. Instead of dwelling on the pain, we can teach our children to trust God. Because of God's unfailing love and grace for His children, He ultimately transforms each painful experience into something that benefits us. As Christians we can have the security of knowing that God will never renege on his promise to make all things work together for good. He never leaves or forsakes us, but promises to give us grace sufficient to meet each trial. Even a young child can understand that God will always be there for us.

Explain that there is never a time limit to God's perfect plan for us. He may bring joy in a day, or it may take several years. We may never fully understand why we experience some painful events, but we can completely trust God to bring us joy through it all. One of the most special gifts a parent can give a child is the example of calm trust in our loving and faithful God.

You may also wish to explore these Scriptures with your child: Romans 8:28; Isaiah 61:3; 1 Thessalonians 5:16–18; James 1:2; and Hebrews 12:9–11.

You can read more about finding joy through pain in my book *Joy That Lasts*.

 **Kari Smalley Gibson** taught elementary school in the inner city of Phoenix, Arizona. Working with children on a daily basis, she decided to write stories that would encourage, comfort, and give hope. Kari now enjoys the slow pace of country living in Branson, Missouri, with her husband, author and speaker Roger Thomas Gibson, and their two children, Michael and Hannah Elise.

 **Richard Bernal's** interest in art began at a young age, when he expressed himself on the chalkboard and desktop. He is now a freelance illustrator who has created illustrations for several children's books, including *Night Zoo* and the award-winning *The Ants Go Marching*. He continues to take art classes to broaden his education, and he often speaks about his work to elementary school children, which he finds an education in itself. He lives in St. Louis, Missouri.